REHSIF

"Where creative writing comes to life to capture the imagination."

Feel free to visit us @ www.rehsif.com

A DAY
IN
THE LIFE
OF
POSITIVITY

By

Wilfred Fisher

2011

Author website: www.rehsif.com

To Taban, My Big Boy

Thank you for being an amazing son and a great brother to your sister. You bring me joy. I treasure our time and experiences. You are loving, smart, thoughtful, talented, respectful, polite and funny. I am so proud of you. My love for you is unconditional. I love you son.

To Mel, My Dearest Princess

You are such a wonderful daughter and a great sister to your brother. You have shown so much courage, strength, will and determination. You are smart and funny. Your smile brightens my day. You fill my heart with so much joy. I love you dearly.

Acknowledgement

I have learned that no one walks alone in life's journey. Life is an incredible journey, and I must thank those who have helped me along the way. First, I want to thank the creator for the many blessings. To my parents, Mr. Wilfred Fisher and Mrs. Linda Fisher, you guys have been instrumental and helpful in so many ways. I could not begin to thank you enough for all that you both have done for me. I love you.

To my sisters Rebeca and Leicest, I love and thank you for your support. To my brother Wegener, it has been a journey, but we both continue to strive. You are a devoted family man and brother. Even though, you are the youngest, there is so much that I have learned from you. Continue teaching and helping the many lives that you come in contact with.

A big thank you to my nieces, Shania, Tatiyana, Tamiya, Sariah, Elyshah and nephew Josiah. You guys are the best and uncle loves you very much. To my In-laws Mr. Mark James and Mrs. Kia Fisher, thank you.

7

To my uncles Fernando, Fons and James for always being there and guiding me with endless advice. You guys showed me that with hard work, all is possible, but most importantly, for reinforcing the importance of remaining humble and keeping a positive perspective on life. Thank you so very much for all the words of encouragements. I love you guys.

I also want to extend my gratitude to these family members. Jessica, you'll always be my sweetie pie. Damany keep that ambitious mindset. Shana, my Rudy Pooh, thanks for granting me the joy of being a Godfather. Amir, I love you. Jamilla keep your face in those books. Vielka, it's remarkable that after not seeing each other for many years, we were able to re-connected, and not missed a beat. I love you V. Selma, Jas, Maria and the rest of my west coast family. Also, to all my other family members whom I have failed to mention, know that I did not purposely mean to do so. I love each and every one of you.

To my friends, Sharan Bruce, Everton Reid, Julio Garibaldi, Angela Hill, Schaunda Chase, Del

Smith, Malika Jones, Yolanda Scott, Alice Teffian, Janice McLean and Robert Headly. Thank you for your positive contributions of love and support.

To my teachers, professors, mentors, and all the supportive souls, who have influenced and continue to contribute to my growth as a man. Many blessings and I positively thank each and every one. Lets all work together towards this positive movement.

"You may have good intentions,
but if your actions are not in alignment with your
thoughts, the outcome may contradict the good in you."

Introduction

This book is meant to uplift, inspire and stimulate all who cross its path by means of positivity. Life has different paths, and they are not always going to be favorable, but it is essential to remain focus and maintain ones dignity, strength, optimism and hope that if focus on positive actions, it will lead to a day in the life of positivity.

I have lived many of the written words in this book. In writing this book, it has had a therapeutic effect on me. This book provided me with an outlet, where I was able to freely express and share my thoughts. It enlighten me on how to be selfless by not only thinking of self, but to think and serve others in love, the same way others have served and helped me to love.

The manifestation of this book started, when I first recognized and acknowledged living a day in the life of positivity. I saw the effect that positive living began to have on me, and on the life of those who I touched. Ever since that special day, I have made a conscious effort to continue living this life, because it's one that has opened many doors. Positive thinking carries an enormous impact. Positivity allows people to tap into their inner resources, so that they can experience the best in them.

As I have and will continue to say, life is a journey, and at one time or another, we all in some capacity will require the help of others to make it through this incredible journey we call life. We help each other by encouraging, praising, assisting, forgiving, giving, sharing, and loving. My hope is that some of the positive words in this book can be a tool that leads some into positive thinking.

I have learned that by replacing negative thoughts with positive thoughts can positively help remove the enormous burden that negativity can weigh on our souls. Learn to dig deep to uncover your hidden positive resources. Replacing negativity with positivity can be a stress reliever. Be inspired to seek positive wording through the many pages of this book.

As you read through the many pages of this book, you will see that I repeated some of my thoughts, and that was solely for the purpose of reinforcement. In reinforcing and affirming positivity, we validate and uphold a positive state.

I can't reach everyone, but in the some that my words touch, I wish to share so that you too can discover the positive potential within your soul. Once you learn and discover the magical powers of positive thinking, share it with others, so that they too can better help themselves. We are all in this together; so despite your circumstances, you should attempt to incorporate positive thinking into your daily life. It all starts with you, and a day in the life of positivity. Conquer life, a day at a time. Remember, in all that you do, keep it positive. Positivity, peace and blessings to all.

with love,

Wilfred Fisher

A DAY IN THE LIFE
OF POSITIVITY

Positivity starts with you

If you are curious about becoming a better you, a great start would be to learn to feel good about yourself.

Curiosity is part of life, and we are all students of life. We seek to define the meaning of our purpose on this earth. We do this from the moment we are born to our last day on earth. Sometimes we ask ourselves, if it's essential to live life in a fulfilling way, or if it's barely enough to get by? Whether we know it or not, we all have a purpose, a meaning, and we are defined by our character.

As human, we define life with each breath that we take, since breathing validates the fact that we are living. Each day that we are alive is a blessing. We should be grateful for each day that we are alive to experience. Life is a breath of fresh air, and we contribute with our daily productivity.

A positive outlook to our existence is validated by our action. We are inspired and encouraged to believe in all that's good. With a peaceful mind, loving soul and genuine heart, we can conquer all that leads to an extra-ordinary life. Staying positive is key and critical to opening many doors. Know that there will be obstacles along the way, but in faith, we can concentrate our attention in living our dreams. Do not be afraid to dream, since it gives us hope.

Dream, open your eyes, and look deep in the mirror. You should be paying attention to what you see in the mirror. What do you see? Do the words confidence, adoration, appreciation, determination, dedication, perseverance and love look familiar? If at first, you don't see it, look again. Those words constitute a compact description of describing the individual in you. Your exterior is like a synopsis, while your interior is the full content of what's inside of your book. You will not be understood unless, others read your book. Also, take the time to read and understand your book. You are all that's inside of your book. When you see all those wonderful words and more, ensure to accentuate and let them shine.

With so much good in you, share it with others by allowing them to read. In doing so; you will reap all the benefits of your benevolent nature. Don't compare yourself to anyone else and ensure to take the time to recognize the beauty in you. We are all beautiful in our own way, so don't be a duplicate of anyone else. We are originals, because we are one of a kind.

Know and remind yourself of how wonderful you are. Don't give in to procrastination and start to feel good about self now. Let this day be the end to your curiosity about improvement and the beginning to a great start to learning the positive in you. Positivity starts with you.

Positivity is in you, not because I said so, but because it is so. Understand that, there are lots of good reasons to feel positive about self. Be thankful for another day and grateful for what you have. Today is another day and an opportunity to live out your dreams. In life, we have all done remarkable things, and you are no exception. Love yourself unconditionally and know that you are undoubtedly and positively blessed. In knowing that you are blessed, is reason enough to feel good about yourself.

Early morning Positivity

Life's gifting makes this a great morning and the beginning to a greater week. It's an opportunity at redemption and a chance to start out new. A chance to expand learning and show thanks for life's many blessings. Don't be afraid to take on new challenges and embrace all that's positive. Greatness awaits, but it takes trying to get there. Once you get on board, you can enjoy the journey. Keep hope and continue loving.

Life is the biggest of gift, and it is important to cherish each and every day. A new day brings light and hope. It is an opportunity for redemption. This new day can be the beginning to a fresh and new start. Don't waste a day not educating yourself. Learn all that life blesses us with on a daily basis. Expand your thinking and be receptive to the views of others. With a peaceful mind, loving soul and genuine heart, you can conquer all that leads to an extra-ordinary life. Always give it that extra, and all that seem so ordinary will be more fulfilling. It is essential to give your best in all that you do. In working hard, you show effort and determination. In your daily living, show your love and appreciation by saying thanks to life's blessings.

It is necessary to be a conscious observer of life. While living, we witness a lot. Life is an abundant of love. You can live life seven times over, and still will not see all that life has to offer. Maximize your experiences by living it to the fullest. In doing so, you can enjoy each and every day to the maximum.

Life is meant to be lived, and it begins with you. Open your eyes to all that's beautiful. We live and learn through experiences. Our experiences can be use as a tool to self development, which can be instrumental in our personal growth. Don't be afraid to take on new challenges and embrace all that's positive.

A DAY IN THE LIFE OF POSITIVITY

Our physical existence is defined with each experience.   As human, we experience as we live, and hopefully, that helps us grow into dependable and respectable citizens.   Doing good to others adds to our blessings.   Do good onto others and good will find its way onto you.   If you practice this, you will see an abundant of good come your way.

Life brings about challenges, but they can be overcome with solutions.   Don't be discouraged by a challenge, as there are many means to arrive at a solution.   Whether you decide to get there by motorcycle, bus, train, boat, airplane, skating or walking, open your arms and embrace life's challenges with a positive attitude.   Positivity brings about enlightenment.

In following your path, you allow yourself to reach extra-ordinary heights.   Greatness awaits all who are bold enough to identify and reach out and grab. There is no wrong in trying.   The journey to make it through an experience is an experience within itself. Don't waste any more time wishing to live that extraordinary life.   Your transportation is ready, so please get on board on life's positive ride; this ride will have you full of hope and love.

Believing in self is Positive

"Believe it, and then you'll see it. Believe that you can by thinking and affirming Positivity. That image change on the inside will be shown and displayed on the outside. Life is so much better when you keep it Positive."

When you have been beat down long enough, believing in yourself may seem so far-fetched. Please, do not get stuck in society's negative patterns. Some people in your life may not have confidence in you, but you should not allow their views to dissuade you from believing in yourself. Do not give them that much power to take over you. Believe in yourself, and you will be able to climb many mountains. Your sense of belief starts with the optimization of your self-esteem and self-acceptance.

Everyone has many different strengths, skills and unique talents. In being unique, makes us so much more alike. When our self-esteem is low, we magnify all that may seem wrong. Our self-acceptance is at its lowest point. We accomplish this by creating mental images in our heads that focuses on our negatives. Instead of thinking on all that may be negative, focus on all that is positive. The responsibility in focusing on all that's positive falls on you. You have to learn to re-channel your thoughts into believing that you can. Once you believe, you will then be able to see it.

There are so many things that we all do well. Ensure to do self-affirmation and remind yourself that you are brilliant, magnificent, superb, glorious, smart, and splendid. Remember that others believe in you, when you believe in yourself. We all have an inner path that enables us to discover the essence of our being. We live in a world that has a wide range of cultural, political, and religious concepts, to name a few. Life throws us curves in the form of triumphs, trials and tribulations, but in the midst of it all, it is essential to maintain a positive outlook on life.

A day in the life of positivity is a way to start channeling positive thoughts into positive action. Thoughts are the images that we carry and have in the inside, while our action is what will be displayed on the outside. You can get into a state of positive consciousness by seeing the positive in things. Once you see the positive light, it can give you the power to recognize and block all that can be viewed as negative. In having the wisdom to recognize and carry out positivity, you can live and experience life from a positive perspective. Use your mental brainpower to stimulate and enlighten others, so they too can be empowered into a positive movement that reciprocates teaching and learning. Know that you can and shall experience life from a positive perspective. You have to trust your instincts and create your path that will lead you on track.

WILFRED FISHER

Once you believe it, you can then see it. Foresee, manifest and it'll become evident. Open your heart and mind to positive living. Life is better when you keep it positive.

Live in Positive brightness

A lot of negativity out there, that if you allow it to get the best of you, it would drain the living day lights out of you into darkness. So much negative vibes wrongly directed at others, when it should be redirected into Positive vibe since you are in control of your actions. Stop blaming others for your shortcomings and know that Positive thinking is a better option in achieving peace of mind.

A path to brightness is guided by the ability to turn on the positivity switch. Positive energy gives a switch the power to turn any dark day into positive brightness. Brightness is always a better option than living in darkness. Living in darkness means staying in a negative state for far too long, that it may have you living in a state of illusion, instead of a state of reality.

31

Turn the switch from Off (darkness) to the On (brightness) position. Do not allow this world to play games with your mind. Take on this world's positive energy and remind yourself that you are in control. The essence of your existence relies heavily on your ability to transform negativity into positivity. The key to erasing negativity is to spend a day in the life of positivity. Once you acquire and master positive thinking, you are guaranteed not to want to return into living that negative life.

All of us at a time or another have lived or are still living in darkness. There is a lot of negativity out there that can keep one in darkness, as to where we are afraid to express ourselves in fear of getting a negative response. We should not live life in fear. If you allow negativity to continue to drain you into darkness, you will not be able to see the bright light that awaits you. Once you build the courage to break the chains of darkness, you will see a door open that will lead you to complete brightness. Don't be afraid to follow the

A DAY IN THE LIFE OF POSITIVITY

light and enter.   Don't forget to leave negativity at the door and enter with confidence because this brightness lifestyle is a movement that is absolutely positive. Life's journey is determined by our choices.   That is why, it's essential to live and think positive.

We are affected by everything we do.   What happens in life is dependent on the decision that we make.   If you want positive outcome, you must put out positive energy.   Brightness comes with changing negative thoughts into positive thoughts.   It comes with making self happy.   It also comes with the choices that you make.   Make better choices and you will see the positive level increase with each positive act of kindness.

A way to live in positive brightness is to give credit to those who have helped along the way when things are going well.   We are all in this together. Positive brightness also means, not blaming others for personal shortcoming and accepting responsibility for your own actions. Good or bad, know that you can change any negative living in life into positive. Say no to darkness, and yes to brightness. Live in positive brightness and maximize your life by achieving peace of mind.

Positivity impacts everyone

We live in a perfect world with imperfect people. The earth provides us with all that we need, yet many people struggle to fill their need. No need for division, as we are all in this together. Learn to extend a helping hand with an open mind and a loving heart. The many lives that we Positively touch can impact our soul.

By nature, people are imperfect beings, and unlike people, the world is not an imperfect world. The world provides all that we could possibly need to live on a day to day basis. As human beings, we are the imperfect souls who make this world seem unlike the perfect world that it is. Point in case, many people waste and throw food away while many starve. Many people have two, three, and even more coats while others struggle to stay warmly. Many people have spare rooms in their homes, while others don't have a place to lay their heads. Many people are wealthy, while others struggle in poverty. Our attitude should not be that of only thinking of ourselves, but of extending and reaching to impact all those that we can. In having a giving attitude and sharing, we can help each other.

In society, we are so divided without attempting to come together. Our world would be a better place, if we were to extend a helping hand with an open mind and a loving heart. We should understand that we are all in this together. The need to help another person must first start with each and every one of us taking the initiative to give of ourselves. If we each extend to help a single person, everyone will eventually get the help that they need. Helping can and it should be a chain reaction. A sequence of positive actions can impact everyone. We can impact our souls deeply with that one life that we positively touch. Keep in mind that, no help is too little.   Any way that one can help another person, it's a positive contribution towards making that person and your life better and ultimately, this world a better place to live.   In helping others, we help ourselves, and that is the way that life was intended to be.

We live in a simple world made complicated by its people.   Just like the world, we as people are very simple but tend to let our instincts to wonder into complex land.   The yet experience (what has not and still hoping to experience) always seems to peak our interest.   It is always wonderful to dream and hope, until we act out our innermost thoughts.

Do not expect anything to be given or granted to you.   Expect to work hard in all that you set your mind to and through hard work and perseverance, you should reach new heights.   Do not strive for success, since that is limited; strive for greatness, since that is unlimited.

Remember, you are great because you are remarkable in magnitude, inferior to none and certainly distinguished because this world provides us with endless boundaries that are all within reach.

Notice how a single word can make a difference. The word is, "*great*." A single word is pregnant with potential. If you are not ready for the responsibilities of word support ensure to protect yourself by not planting the seed that will flourish, and evolve into a word that will eventually grow. If the word is negative, it may return to haunt you. Words are powerful. It is a good practice to utilize them wisely. Just like when dealing with anyone, you should always lead by example. A good place to start is with self. Also, be true to yourself and others. By teaching one, we can reach and impact many.

Positivity is the seed to greatness

We all have seeds of greatness in us, so plant them.   Don't be stagnant; rise out of complacency. Grow and branch out, as there is no limit to joy or happiness.   Keep reaching for new heights.   Like roots, choose to spread and see a beautiful life from the inside out.   Don't look back or live in the past; your best days are still out in front of you.

As stated at the very beginning of the book, positivity starts with you.   By now, your positive thinking gears should be in motion.   A gear that's positively turning is the start to becoming a better you. It all begins with you.   The seed to greatness is in all of us.   It is crucial to know and believe this.   In knowing that you carry seeds of greatness in you, allows you to identify and understand the importance of properly planting, nourishing and watching your internal seed blossom into positive greatness. Positivity is essential in our daily production. A positive state of mind allows us to grow into the person we are all meant to be. It takes work, but it is worth the labor. Do not remain stagnant and believe that change will occur without action. Rise out of darkness which is complacency and into a bright new life filled with greatness. Let this be the beginning, to a day in the life of positivity.

Life is about many beginnings. There is no conclusion without a beginning. When you start to reach great heights, you should positively express your appreciation with gratitude and love. No one should be exempt from expressing appreciation. Learn to appreciate and express your thankfulness. Don't take for granted the importance and power of a thank you. A nice gesture of love has a tremendous effect on a receptive soul. It does not always take giving something material to express ones gratitude. A single compliment or even a smile can turn someone's entire day all around.

It is a blessing to grow and branch out, as there is no limit to joy or happiness. We all wish to reach that stable place that brings us security and comfort. Like roots, you should choose to spread and see a beautiful life from the inside out. Don't attempt to be anyone else. Be yourself. In all your genuine actions, others will see the beauty within you.

From afar and without knowing, some people like to judge others situation. That is until the tables turn. Know that at some time or another, the tables do turn, since that is the way of the world. It goes round and round. Those same people don't understand that situations are merely a test that we all go through in life. We all have a story to tell, because if we are living life, we will experience many situations. We all have dirt, so it is essential for all of us to humble ourselves to lead a positive life. No one is innocent enough to condemn or judge. Knowing that no one is perfect and that we'll make mistakes along the way, should be reason enough not to be afraid of mistakes and live life with a positive purpose.

Everyone can achieve greatness. How we achieve greatness in our lives, is defined by how we handle adversities. Remember, that no one is on life's journey alone. With the help of those around us like family, friends, neighbors, colleagues, we can overcome adversities. To have the encouragement, advice, and support of love ones is priceless. Adversity develops unknown talents. One talent is to recognize and develop our seed of greatness. Once your positive seed blossom, move ahead, don't look back or live in the past; your best days are still in front of you. Your future should be synonymous with positivity.

Reach out to Positivity

"Like a tree, learn to grow, branch out and share your positive fruits with others." No one should need consent or approval to capture the essence of Positive living. Reach out and grab the fruit that'll fill and nourish your Positive crave. Take in Positive vibe and get full of a day in the life of Positivity.

Capture the essence of positive living. It does not matter if the tree grows apples, pears, peaches, cherries, or strawberries; like a tree, branch out and share all your positive fruits with others. Allow others to grab and eat the fruits that will fill and nourish their positive crave. Positive fruits are in abundance; they are amazing, confident, delightful, dynamic, enticing, excellent, exquisite, flourishing, gracious, good, great, healthy, priceless, precious, radiant and rewarding.

We should always think before saying anything. It is a good practice to think and then speak, as opposed to speaking and then thinking. Before saying anything, we should think positive, because words are a reflection of our thoughts. Positive words come from positive thoughts. Listen to the words that come out of your mouth, as they will give you an idea as to the direction that you will head into. Positive thoughts equate to positive results. Once you acquire the habits of living positively, help others embrace, and experience the essence of capturing positive living. Your direction may lead others into positive fruits of love, joy, peace, kindness, goodness, faithfulness, gentleness, self-control and love. In order to reach others where they currently at, we must first know where we at; that way, we can begin this journey together.

There are those who plant seeds that blossoms into a tree that produces positive fruits, and others who don't know how to plant seeds. For those of you who have mastered the art of planting seeds, please take the time to teach and share your understanding with those around you.   Be a provider of knowledge by helping others in the production of their own positive fruits. Hopefully, those who have embraced learning to produce their own positive fruits, can also embrace the positive energy that will soon follow.

While learning, don't be afraid to reach out and grab a positive fruit from another tree.   You should not be scared.   A positive fruit reaps many benefits.   You should not let pride get the best of you.   At one time or another, we all need help.   Humble yourself to accept from others.

When you find the right fruit, and you decide to bite into it, ensure to get a big bite.   A piece of a positive fruit carries so much positive vibes that you'll be wanting more.   You may develop an addiction to this wonderful fruit, but don't be afraid to be addicted to a positive fruit.   There is no such thing as too much positivity.   The more; the merrier.   Take the time to take in on the positive.   Take many deep breaths and consume on all the positive vibes that mystify in the air. Mother nature provides us with an abundant of love, so make sure to get full of a day in the life of positivity. Get full of positive love and share it with those around you.

Gain Positivity

Maybe not now, but at one time or another, we all needed to be encouraged, and challenged to reach newer heights. It is easy to complain, criticize, judge, condemn, and find fault in others, but our goal should be that of encouraging the best in ourselves and others. Be respectful of others as respect gains trust.

At one time or another, we all need to hear a voice of reason. Whether we hear our inner voice, or that external voice of a family, friend, or stranger speaking to us, we need to hear that positive voice that can help us humble ourselves. That voice can trigger our positive gears into taking it to that next level. Everyone wants to excel, but it is essential to remember that we need to value and put hard work into all that we seek to achieve. In all that we do, we all need help.

A lot of people may have no problem when it comes to helping self, but are a bit hesitant when it comes to helping others. Extend that helping hand and help someone else get off the floor. Helping someone else is not only fulfilling for the receiver, but it is also rewarding for you the giver. No one should have to go on life's journey alone. We are all in this together. The sooner we learn that it takes a joint effort, the sooner we can all gain positivity together.

You have those who never seem to be satisfied. Even when things are going well, many find it in them to complain, criticize, judge, condemn or find faults in others, when they should be encouraging, pushing, and challenging others to newer heights. At one time or another, we all need to dig deep to overcome obstacles, and that can be made easier with the help of others. When someone is trying to reach newer heights, be their motivator that helps them get to the top of that new mountain. When treating others with respect, you help make our world a better place to live.

A DAY IN THE LIFE OF POSITIVITY

Improving relations with others should be at the forefront of those who want to make a conscious effort to lead a prosperous, sharing and peaceful lifestyle. Be kind to each and everyone you meet. Don't allow stereotypes, prejudice or other biases to overtake you. Stand strong and in control. Whether it's a family member, friend, classmate, coworker or stranger, always encourage, push and challenge them to be the best they can be. Try not to complain, criticize, judge or find faults in them. Treat others, the way you would like to have them treat you. Respect should be at the top of your practices. Give out respect to earn respect.

We live in a diverse society made up of many different cultures, languages, races, religions and backgrounds. In understanding diversity, we can make our lives a lot more fun and fascinating, but only if, we find the time to get along by respecting each other. It's crucial to respect other's views and opinions. Try to be respectful and understanding of their feelings. In genuinely helping others, we help build trust, and in them gaining trust, we gain respect.   Always be respectful as respect gains trust.

Organizing is Positive

"It's easy to be overwhelmed when disorganized, but when organized, it's easier to take all in stride." Gather your thoughts, and place them in order of priority. Don't worry about what you can't control, and take a stance on controlling what you can. Affirm your beliefs and believe in what you affirm. Positivity is the best organizer.

Our mind is a powerful tool. It has the ability to think, visualize, store, and place all in perspective. When all is in perspective, we are able to find a way of regarding situations and judge their relative importance in our lives. In organizing our thoughts, we are no longer overwhelmed and are more objective in the way we see our point of view and that of others. Our views become clearer, and that helps us retain and remember.

51

Our mind is our thoughts organizer. Whether we remember something now or later, our mind stores all that comes our way. Even when organized, our mind needs help in reaching great heights. With the help of our environment, the people whom we cross paths with in life, and day by day experiences that we encounter, it all helps us into becoming productive human beings. It is all about learning from our everyday experiences.

Life can be overwhelming at times, but it takes organizing our priorities to ease the over thinking process. Take a moment to take in on all of the beautiful things that life offers us and ponder on your many blessings. Take a deep breath and realize that you are in control of your path. A great first step would be to organize your life.

Living disorganized can add to the overwhelming demand of daily living, and at times, it can hinder a positive progression. A positive progression should always be at the top of the list of things to accomplish. We should not allow others to deter us from positively organizing our lives. In attempting to get organize, you should gather your thoughts, opinion and/or ideas; recognize them for what they are, and put them in order of priorities in your life. Once you accomplish this, you will be able to walk in the path that will lead you into a positive progression. To prioritize is to organize.

Maximize your life and live it to the fullest. Do what you can and don't worry about what you can't control in life. Instead of worrying, you should take a stance on controlling what you can, and get a grip on what needs to be arranged for your life positive progression. Life is all about progression. We live to move forward. Organizing is a step forward in the right direction. Each step that you take is a positive progression. Don't be stagnant and get moving. When moving, believe in yourself by affirming what you believe in. You should be your biggest cheerleader. If you don't believe in yourself, you can't expect anyone else to believe in you. Whether you take baby steps or a massive one, what should be of most importance to you is getting to your destination. In all that you do, stay focus and organize. Positive thinking is the best organizer.

A Positive starring role

In life, we all hold a starring role in a movie called, "My Life." In life, we merely share the stage with many other stars. No need for power struggles since everyone is a star. We just happen to be the biggest of stars in our own life, so play that starring role well since you are the one who benefits the most. Act your part and make your movie the best it can be. A great start would be with a great and Positive attitude.

In life, we get the opportunity to watch series, sitcoms, sports, news, documentaries, and even movies, but life is the greatest acting job that anyone could have. Life allows us to play out our own movie. It just happens that, the main star of the movie is you. In your life, you are not able to sit and watch your movie unfold. You must live and feel this movie's way from beginning to end. Every movie has a beginning (birth) and an ending (the day we leave earth). You are solely responsible for filling in the gap in between by maximizing your potential. You are the star who holds the starring role. In addition, you are also the director, producer, and writer. Take advantage of your opportunities, as you are responsible for making your movie, the best it can be.

In life's path, we share the stage along the way with many stars, but the direction that one takes in life will be determined by the actions taken on the movie stage. There will be many who wish to be the lone star in their movie, but they fail to realize that every movie needs a supporting cast. Just like in life, we always require that support to help us excel. When we excel, we transcend. Transcending is a sign of doing well. Keep everything in perspective and understand that even when doing well, there are still millions of stars in the world. Each star may stand out in its own movie,

but no one star is more significant than the other.
Every day, a star is born.   At times, it may be difficult
distinguishing between stars, but it does not hurt to
attempt to identify.

In this wonderful world, we all have the
potential (standing still but ready) to shine, but we need
to put it into operation by utilizing our kinetic (moving
motion) power that places it into action.   The sky is a
big stage, and there is more than ample room in the sky
to allow each and every star to stand alone and shine.
Respect others space and feeling.   Allow them all to
shine in their own unique way.   We are all here to
inspire and motivate each other into achieving and
reaching extra-ordinary heights.   No need for power
struggles since we all hold a starring role in our own
movie called, "My Life."   We merely share the stage
with many other stars.   Remember everyone is a star.
You are just the biggest star in your life.   Play this
starring role well, since you are the one who benefits
the most from making this movie the best it can be.   A

great start to accomplishing this would be to have a great and positive attitude.

Life's Positive gift

Wake up to another wonderful day. Take a deep breath and consume life's gift. Listen to your heart beat Positive vibes. Feel the Positive energy reflecting on longevity. Seize the moment and acknowledge your blessings. Another day to give it a go. A chance to help another soul. An opportunity to achieve a goal. Take the time to be thankful in voice and action for the gift of life.

In life, we all have a purpose and whatever that purpose is, it is essential to do it with passion. Quit looking at all that's wrong in life and begin to be grateful for all that's right. There is so much more right than there is wrong. Your life may not be perfect, but as imperfect as it may seem, there is someone out there who would love to trade places with you. That someone may think that your shoe may look mighty good on them.   Negative thinking brings about stress. Help to reduce stress by eliminating negative self-talk. Learn to be happy where you are and passionately find the enthusiasm to pursue life's gifting.

Remind yourself that today will be another wonderful and lovely day.   This day will be wonderful and lovely because you said it, so it shall be.   No better day, than this wonderful day.   Reinforce your belief and believe in what you say.   You can do that by carrying and acting out all that you profess.   Take a deep breath and slowly inhale the positivity in the air. Inhale all that you can.   Each breath of air that you consume is life's most glorious gift.   Have a grateful attitude and recognize that this day is a gift, so unwrap it by loving and living positively.   Despite your circumstances, keep the joy in your heart.   Continually work on becoming a better individual.   Choose to be kind to those around you.   Learn to love without limits or exception.   If you haven't already done so, let today be the beginning to finding ways to be passionate about life.   It all starts today.   It all starts now.

Positivity is displayed with action, so act accordingly and show off your positive energy.   We are what we continuously say and do.   If we look at life from a half-empty perspective, as opposed to half-full can play an integral role in how we live life.   Our views are influential, since the way we think reflects our outlook on life.   Think positive, so you can feel positive.   Begin to feel terrific about self and change self image into believing positively.   An optimistic view on life does not only help us mentally, but it can also have an enormous impact with our health.

We can view life from a pessimistic point of view, but do not be discouraged and keep hope alive because optimism is never too far away.   With a few mental tweaking, we can program our positive thinking, and that can be made feasible with optimism. Remember that positive thinking is a skill that can be

learn and taught.   Learn to embrace positive living.
Know that you can learn it, and once you do, ensure to
do your part by keeping the cycle going of teaching it to
someone who may need to be enlighten.

There is no such thing as the perfect time to
seize a positive moment.   Opportunities always present
itself.   It's up to you to acknowledge and act according
to what's best in your life.   Take on this moment and
start being positive now.   There is no better time than
now.   Take on this moment to acknowledge each and
all your blessings.   In helping another soul, you
multiply the many blessings.   Use your voice to share
your insight and show life's gratefulness with the gift of
positivity.

Another Positive gifting

Every day is a new gifting.   We open our gifts with the opening of our eyes.   Wake up to this new day. Exhale negativity and inhale on all the Positive that this lovely day brings.   Another day to be thankful for the opportunity to try again.   Take on this day with confidence and don't waste another minute not taking advantage of your opportunities.   Know that you can, and you will.   Life is undeniably good.

Open your eyes, and say hello to reality. Living is real, but most importantly, our existence is life most precious gift.   Take on life as it comes to you. Accept all the good that life offers in stride, and turn all that may be seen as bad into good with your positive outlook.   Having a positive perspective on life can be a transforming life experience.   Embrace all that's good.

63

A positive outlook is overall productive. Turn all that comes your way into good all around. A new day brings about another positive gifting. Every day that we are able to open our eyes is a gifting. We unwrap and open our gifts with the opening of our eyes. Be thankful, for the gift of life. Show your gratitude with the actions that you make throughout this day. Our action determines our direction, and our deeds validate our character. Self respect and confidence can shape our character. No one can guide you into good character but you. Your character can differentiate you from others. It is what makes an individual, an individual. In building confidence, you can internally build yourself as a whole, while externally helping others with your positive vibe that will radiate onto them. Make sure to live right and lead a healthy life by doing well to self and others.

There is so much to look forward to living. If not prepared, it can be overwhelming. Calm yourself to be able to take on all that this world has to offer.

A DAY IN THE LIFE OF POSITIVY

Before taking on the world, ensure to exhale on all that
is negative, and inhale on all that is positive. Meditate
on clearing your mind of toxic information and starting
out new with productive knowledge that can be
communicated and shared with others. Reemphasizing
and reinforcing the importance of sharing, as it is caring
to do for another fellow man kind. We are all in this
together. No one should ever have to feel or be alone
in life's journey. Remember, life is a gift, and it is to
be shared with others, and life's journey is incredible
when it's traveled with other souls. Travel in joy and
embrace all the positivity that this day certainly brings.

Today is your huge opportunity to do all that
you have wished to do. Do not procrastinate on doing
today, what you wished you had done yesterday. If
you have unsuccessfully tried to do something in the
past, today is your opportunity to try once again.
Don't ever give up. Take on this day with confidence,
and don't waste another minute not taking advantage of
your opportunities. Know that you can take advantage

of your opportunities.   Tell yourself that you will, and you will be on your way.   Life is undeniably good.

Closing in on Positivity

"Every failure leads you one step closer to your goal. In failing, it proves that you have tried. In trying, it proves that you took a step. In taking a step, it will help you get closer. In getting closer, your goal gets within reach. In reaching, you exude Positivity. In being Positive over shadows failure. Failing is not an option, but trying is."

Opting for your goal is positive all around. Think positive and don't ever be afraid of failure. Stay focus on positivity and do not allow failure to prevent you from seeking greatness. Instead of looking at failure from a negative point of view, know that every failure leads you, one step closer to your positive goal. The only way to close in on positivity is to try by taking steps. In trying, you get within reach of your goals.

In reaching, you certainly exude positivity because you show motivation. Be motivated enough to set your goals and work hard to get all that you wish to achieve. Achievement will over shadow failure.

On your initial attempt to greatness, you may fail, but it should not stop or deter you from continuing. As individuals, we should all have a cause and should never give up. Giving up should not be an option. You should always strive for improvement in your life and the world that you live. In this world, we are all shareholders, and it is important for us all to contribute to making this world the best it can be.

Pay close attention to this Landlord-Tenant analogy; because some people live their daily life doing things, while others take. We should work hard on wanting to be landlords of our space, and not merely be happy occupying space as tenants. Tenants tend to be complacent and stagnant to the idea of not doing anything. Tenants occupy space, while not being

A DAY IN THE LIFE OF POSITIVITY

responsible for anything within their space.   As
landlords, one has a sense of awareness.   A landlord
knows that they are responsible for theirs and everyone
else's space.   Landlords work on improvement.
They take on the responsibility to fix all that is broken,
maintain and find ways to improve.   A landlord
objective is to make things better.   The landlord-tenant
analogy is similar to the way many live life.   To lead a
productive life means making stride for improvement.
We live to learn, and we learn as we live.

In the eyes of some, failure is viewed as
negative when their initial action doesn't show signs of
immediate results.   In the eye of others, failure is
viewed as positive particularly when the result helps
them get closer to their goals.   When getting closer,
one should appreciate and take a look at their
surrounding and learn from the experience.   Extend
yourself as you get within reach, and grab on to your
goal.   Appreciation and thankfulness should not be

overlooked.   When you learn, share your positive experience by teaching others that one only fails when they don't try.   One must try, try, try.   Trying is a better option than just standing still.   If you don't make a move, you will not reach your destination.   Get going and get moving.   Capture the essence of all that's positive and close in on positive living as living is positive.

Hold on to Positivity

Have you ever held on to something or someone so tight, but knew deep inside, that you should have opened your hands and let go?   Learn when to let go. Let go of feelings of hate, jealousy, regret, and anything or anyone toxic.   Embrace and know that you are worth unconditional love, happiness, joy and an abundance of Positive vibe.

Like everything else in life, there is a flip side to all that's defined as good.   There is the cruelty, selfishness, disappointment, pain, evilness, the fear of death and life's misleading paths.   Do not allow these negative thoughts to consume your positive state. These are all things in our thoughts that can trigger a chain reaction from our action, so we try hard not to externally verbalize our train of thought.   Some of these thoughts never get worded because of fear of how it may be viewed by others.

Living in fear is not the healthiest way to live. When we love ourselves and others, we minimize fear. We should not allow fear to be the reason why we confine our thoughts to our mind. We should share and not have to be afraid to reveal many of our actual thoughts. When we sit back and think on all that we think about, we can see that in every good or bad thought, whether we agree or disagree about the same thoughts, we can honestly say that it all defines the meaning and purpose of life.

When we forgive, we remove resentment. Resentment is baggage. Forgiveness removes a burden off us. These deep feelings could consume us if we don't learn to let it go, so open your hands and let it go. Give yourself options. People love options. Options gives us a sense of pride and a freedom of choice. The power that we get in having the right to choose is empowering in its own way. We should allow honesty to be the new trend setter towards truthfulness. To be honest is to be forthright and free. Freedom is incredible.

Love is full of surprises, and it can motivate anyone to do many things. Ensure to take it all in stride and act accordingly. There are many ways for one to love. At the end of the day, love is loving. Love can persuade anyone to do many crazy things, but it is essential to stay focus and maintain a positive outlook. Love is intense. It is a feeling of deep affection. Love is not negative, abusive, insulting or harmful. Love is positive, caring, nurturing and protective. Love is not something that it's clearly defined by many, but it is something that we all want and need.

When it comes to love, there is no need for guessing. You will know when you love. Love is both action and feeling, so when the action is shown, the feeling grows. There is no need to settle, because love provides for endless hope. There is no better option than love. When you love, say it. When you love, show it. Don't expect anything but remain open, as love can be reciprocated. Love unconditionally without fears. Realize that love can be lost. Love is great. Love is positive.

Love can define our lives by giving it meaning. Family, friends, relationship, or even our faith in God are all pivotal factors for many to determine and define their true level of happiness, of inner peace of soul and mind, feelings of harmony and enjoyment of giving and/or receiving. They allow and give meaning to our existence. We all believe in something. Whatever that something may be, it is defined by us. Again, remind yourself to let go. Let go of feelings of hate, jealousy, regret, and anything or anyone toxic. Embrace and know that you are worth unconditional love, happiness, joy and an abundance of positive vibes.

Impact the world Positively

Words should not be used to describe a negative situation; they should be used to change the situation. Put your words into action.   Remember, words are powerful, so use them wisely to impact our world Positively.

In any word that one chooses to verbalize, we can in many ways profoundly affect a family member, spouse, companion, friend, colleague, or even a stranger.   We always speak of first impression, but last impression is just as powerful.   In a lifetime, people get many opportunities to make an impression.   They just don't get the chance to make a first or last impression twice.   So take advantages of your opportunities, and choose your words wisely.   In many instances, some people walk away with the baggage of leaving without closure. Last impressions are final. When given the chance, ensure to keep the line of communication open, so that no word can be left without an explanation and understanding.

The ability to communicate plays an integral role in our world. One of the major ways that we use to communicate is with the power of words. The power of words can be extremely powerful. Whether spoken or written, words have the power to transform our lives. Words have a more significant meaning, when it is used to inspire others into being the best they can be, as opposed to when they are used to demean or insult others. When using words, we should not use them to describe a negative situation; they should be used to change the situation. Many are afraid of change, so they are comfortable in remaining stagnant to what they know. Change is not always a negative thing. When used and placed into action, change can be positive. This happens when we use positive action to turn a negative into something entirely positive.

A DAY IN THE LIFE OF POSITIVITY

In some of life's experiences, a word can drag a person down into depression, and at other times, it can uplift a person into elation. Some choose to use words to harm some, while others opt to heal broken or damaged hearts. You are the one who decides what it is that you wish to do with the words that you know. In the way that you express yourself, do it with an open and loving heart. Treat others, the way that you would wish and want others to treat you. We must show respect, if we want others to respect us. We are all in this journey together. In understanding the importance of word usage, you can begin in the process of being sympathetic towards others.

Try not to convince yourself into believing that it's all about you, and understand that, you are a piece to the world puzzle that helps in the collaboration of something big and helpful. Words can be use to inform, communicate, help, persuade, ease pain, comfort, and love to name a few. The real power of words can help us by motivating, inspiring, comforting and encouraging us to help ourselves and others reach newer heights. A word can be significantly powerful in helping many lives move forward, and it can also be detrimental in the progression if one does not understand its timing. A wise person does not always find the right words to say, at the right time, but they allow the unsaid to remain unsaid at a time when they are tempted to say what shouldn't be said. Remember, words are powerful, so use your words wisely to impact our world in a positive way.

Positivity helps focus

"A Positive state of mind does not remove all the problems in your life, but it does help in keeping you focus to be able to address and solve your life's problems."

In life, we will encounter many problems; that, we can't avoid.   There are ups, down, and in between, when it comes to life experiences.   Live, learn, and take notes along the way.   Life is a journey, so stay focus in your travels.   Know where you are going, and if unsure, get a map that will lead you on the right track. Knowledge is key to reaching enormous heights.

When I speak of a map, I am not physically referring of the paper that contains drawings and directions.   The map I am referring to is the one available to lead you right.   The right track is a positive state of mind, and even if it takes you three left turns to arrive at this state, it will be worth your while to have reached on the right track.   Know that, this is not a track sprint, and there is no set time to arrive.   It is ok to walk.   Take the time to review your map.   A map may be in the form of a person, computer, books or any other resource where you can get the information required to arrive.   We all arrive to a positive state of mind at different times, but what's important; it's that we eventually arrive.   Once you arrive, it does not mean that you stop there; it means to remain focused with the information attained.   Use the information to reach newer heights.

A positive state of mind does not remove all of life's problems, but it does help in dealing with the day by day issues that we encounter in life.   There are no promises made when it comes to life, but one thing is certain, while living, we should maximize life's value by living it to the fullest.

A DAY IN THE LIFE OD POSITIVITY

Life can and is beautiful when we work at it.
There are many factors that contribute to our happiness,
and to us having a sound mental state of mind.
Positivity is a leading contributor.   Feed your mind all
the positive reinforcement that it needs.   Think of the
smile that you can help place on someone else face or
the good deed that you can do for someone else.   If it's
the job that you have, thinking of a loved one, a passion
you have, the visit to the salon, gardening, comedy
show, bowling, swimming, or the sound of music that
make you smile, then by all means, think of those
positive things.   Do not restrict yourself from thinking
of pleasant memories, but don't stop there, work on
creating new ones and if you can, combining the old
and new to create greater experiences.

My thoughts are made out of many of the words
that are scrambled within my mind.   My adrenaline is
driven by my thoughts.   This time around, I have
gathered the words and made it into a poem.   Enjoy the
poem, and hopefully you can get something out of it.

Sound Full Mind

The sound of life wakes me

and with the opening of the eye,

I unwrap the gift of this day.

Life's melody is music to my ears

and to be able to listen to today's song is indeed,

a miraculous blessing.

I yawned my troubles away, and now,

I dance to the rhythm of the musical tune.

With a stable mind and loving heart,

I embrace all that's humbly productive.

Alive and thankful I stand, and now,

I am able to see this day unfold with peace of mind.

===

Allowing my mind to roam into positive land, helps me stay focus.   Whatever means helps you stay on track, use it to arrive at a positive destination.   Once at your positive destination, continue reinforcing positive thoughts into a positive state of mind.

Move towards Positivity

You may not be where you should be, but at least you're not where you used to be.   Quit being hard on yourself.   As long as you're doing your best, you don't have to live in regret.

Stop postponing happiness, and the belief that one day you'll be happy, if you accomplish specific goals first.   The perfect time to be happy is not tomorrow, it is now.   A positive and happy future begins right where you are at, then moving forward. Start taking steps now.   Being happy is a choice, and it is essential to make a conscious effort to lead and live a happy life.   This all starts with you.

You may not be where you want to be because of believing that you'll be happy once you achieve certain goals.   It is not fair to suspend happiness until finding that perfect mate, having that first child, buying that first fancy car, paying off those credit cards bill, finding that perfect job, or losing a certain amount of weight.   These are things that can be accomplished with time and effort, so one should not use these as a reason not to be happy.   Stop placing so much time and energy thinking on the things you may not have, and spend more time thinking of the things you are blessed to have.   Focus on your strengths, and not your weaknesses.   When we criticize ourselves, we delay our growth.   Always know that you are never alone.

Life's journey is a joint venture.   It takes everyone contribution to make this world what it is. The world will continue to go round and round.   With other helpful souls, life is made easier.   You can either be that gravitating vibe that draws people to you to move forward, or you can be that one that gravitates and learn from others in the hope of reaching that joyous destination.   It is a give and take situation.

A DAY IN THE LIFE OF POSITIVITY

At times, we tend to look back and start regretting many of the decisions that we have made in life. That should not be the way to live. We should look at life for what it is, "a journey." Remember that if you had the opportunity to return in time and make changes, those changes may lead you into a destination that you may not be ready to explore. Keep in mind that wanting change does not guarantees tranquility. Altering life's path can lead into unknown and unwanted territories. Even though, life does not always takes us where we want to go, we should be thankful that we are getting the option to choose. In life, we will always make mistakes, so brace yourself to accept your mistakes and move on. We are not always going to experience right. We will also experience so much wrong. Do not be discourage. Learn from your mistakes and live life to the fullest.

Experiences should teach us to learn. We learn by experiencing. In attempting to change the course of life, does not guarantee that if the opportunity arise, you would be alive at that time to see all that you hope to see. Taking chances is part of life, but there is always right and wrong to all that we wish to take a chance. It is on you to reap the benefits of all the incredible things that are out there and to leave behind all that is not. So don't be hard on yourself for doing wrong and continue focusing on doing right. If you continue doing right, it will all pay off in time. Allow your right choices to lead you towards life's positive path.

Positive perception

We are equipped to do as we please, but always too afraid to be ourselves.   We allow others opinion to re-direct us into living life their way.   Don't live life through the eyes of others.   Don't be afraid to follow your own heart and intuition, they somehow already know what you truly want to do.   Positive perception guides you in the right direction.

Confidence should not be dependent on others opinion but on your own acceptance.   Let other's opinion and perception roam within their mind and not take control of your thoughts.   There are things in life that we are not able to explain or even come to that conclusion rationally.   When rational, we are able to exercise our ability to reason.   A sound mind is key to being in tuned with our intuitive senses.   Our intuition is that feeling of mystery, that gut feeling or instinct that often turns out to be right at the end. In knowing without words, or sensing the truth without explanations is a way that we display our intuitive ways. Whether dealing with the past, present, or future, our intuition can be a driving force. Use that force to lead you towards joy, love, honor, respect, happiness, forgiveness, sharing, understanding, or even kindness.

We all have an archive of good in us. It is on you as an individual, to tap into your subconscious mind and trust your intuition of goodness. When good thoughts come to mind, let it out and act on all that goodness that is in you. Just because, someone is not readily able to articulate something at that time, does not mean that their point may not be valid. We are all able and equipped to do anything, but too afraid to be ourselves. Being true to self is of the utmost importance. We need to understand self before even attempting to understand anyone else.

A DAY IN THE LIFE OF POSITIVITY

We allow others opinion to re-direct us into living life their way, but it is on us to have an understanding of how to live life our way.   In life, we always have many available choices.   Once you become self conscious of the fact that there are aspects of your life that are not making you happy, you should make the choice to make changes by take action.   In taking positive action, you can begin to start turning things around.

Many at times, we often find ourselves going through life on autopilot.   Take control and don't allow your life to be in cruise control.   We go through the motion and allow each passing day to be just like the previous.   Learn to break out of this cycle and follow your dreams.   Find the courage and dare to be different.   All the necessary tools needed are within you.   You are in charge of your path and life.   Once you are able to uncover your inner strength which we all have, you can then discover all the tools that are within you.

We are not perfect, but it is essential to experience and learn from those experiences. We will make mistake along the way, so do not be afraid to follow your own heart and intuition. Your heart and intuition already seem to know what you want. Trust and believe in yourself.

Positivity makes a great impact

Regardless of status or where one is in life, it is ok to greet, smile, listen, help, and even forgive others. Never make anyone feel insignificant or inferior. It's the simple thing that makes such a great impact in someone else's life. Minimize stress and maximize love by keeping it Positive.

The simple things in life can make such a tremendous impact in someone's life. At times, the effect of a simple thing is more than one could imagine. We should not take for granted the power of a positive deed or gesture. It is not always about doing major things, but about doing the things that are significant in someone else's life like greeting, smiling, embracing, listening, helping, or even forgiving others for wrong doing. Regardless of status, or where you are in life,

91

one should not think of anyone as being inferior. We are all in this life journey together, so it is essential to be of help to others, and in helping others, we help ourselves. Focus on being one who gives of themselves, more so than one who likes to take from others. Be a giver, and not solely a taker.

As high as one may think that they are on the status list, there are things and/or circumstances that can quickly humble us down to reality. Life takes us through ups and down. Know that when standing high, it only takes one experience to bring you down. Check yourself by leaving the negative attitude behind and don't wait for adversity to do it for you. A voluntary act is more fulfilling than one that is forced your way. Don't wait for adversity to force you into doing right by others. Make sure to treat others, the way you would want others to treat you. Respect is something that we are always taught that is earned. Respect yourself and others along your way, and you will see others respect you with each act of kindness.

A DAY IN THE LIFE OF POSITIVITY

In all that you do, ensure to put out positive energy. Allow your positive vibe to impact those whose path you cross. Life can take us through some turns, and at times, it can take us through unexpected turn of events that can change our lives around. Be grateful for all of the incredible things that life offers, but do not live with a chip on your shoulders. Some of life's unexpected wonders such as hurricanes, blizzards, tornadoes, earthquakes can quickly take away many of the material values that place one on a high status. Remember that after all of the material things that one can have goes, the one thing that does stay behind is character. Work on your character on a daily basis, because that is one thing that no one can take away from you.

Learn to control what you can and don't worry about what you can't control. Be respectful of everyone and regardless of where one is in life, don't stop where you are at. Work hard to self improve, and advance yourself into being the best you can be. Your positive impact is measured with the positive work that you put out.   Minimize stress and maximize love by keeping it positive.

Fill your soul with Positivity

"Don't worry about what they should do, do what you can do. Don't worry about what they know; learn what you need to know. Don't worry about they not loving you, learn to love yourself. Calmly learn to fill your soul with Positivity that'll reassure you of the Positive soul that rest within you."

Don't worry about what everyone else is doing. Try to focus more on what it is you need to do to improve. Be constructive with your development and don't allow it to be compulsive, as to where you lose track of your direction. Stay focus and keep your constructive objective on the forefront of things to do. Many get caught up in focusing on other people's achievement, instead on focusing on what they need and can achieve for themselves. Work on a plan that will elevate you to the next phase of your journey. Life has a whole lot to offer, and it is up to you to optimize. Once you realize this, use what life offers to achieve maximum results. Don't lose hope based on what others tell you that you can't do. Believe in yourself, and know that saying, "I can't" should not be an option. One should always try and not allow someone else to fill their soul with anything but positive wording. It is not against the law to work hard for what you want. Goals can be achieved if we put in the required work. In putting in the work, you can see your life reach levels never before imagined. Believe in your dream, and you will see that it will all come to be. Positive reinforcement is positive, positive, positive all around. I am emphasizing positive.

Don't worry about what others know and focus on what you should know. What you know, it's more significant to you than what others know. Knowledge and understanding helps in ones growth. "We grow when we learn, and we learn when we grow." Take a moment to digest this last quote and try to understand it if you haven't already done so. We grow as people with the things that we learn on a day by day basis, and we learn as people with our willingness to be open minded enough to embrace growth on all levels.

It is ok to respect others for what they know, but don't be in awe because you too can learn what they know if you apply yourself into learning and studying. You should not be intimidated by what you too can achieve. Do things because you wish to do it and not because you see others doing it. Everything can be mastered if we apply ourselves into repetition. If at first one does not succeed, it is essential to try to work at it again and eventually, you can get to the level that you had wished to get. Rote memory works if we study something enough. Rote learning can be used to build a knowledge foundation. Any knowledge attained facilitates understanding, and understanding is a key factor to knowing that you don't have to worry about what anyone else knows because of you knowing what you know.   Knowledge is your foundation.

Don't worry about anyone not loving you, because as long as you love yourself, others will recognize genuine love.   In others recognizing genuine love, it will eventually return your way.   In life, everything is a cycle as everything seems to come back in full circle.   Be patient by calmly learning to fill your soul with positivity that'll reassure you of the positive soul that rest within you.

Don't wait on Positivity

Understand that, when saying, "I'll leave it in God's Hands" does not mean stand still and wait. One must assist by being a contributor to the cause. Be his best helper and believe that it'll come to fruition. Be a doer and stop waiting for things to happen. Do your part and you shall receive. Positive actions bring about Positive results.

Understand that, when standing still, much does not get done. To accomplish positivity, we must make an effort to go in that direction. Life is about choices and making decisions, so you should decide on where you want to go. Be active and make things happen. Don't just be one to say much, but be the one who does a whole lot more. Even though, we are not in life's journey alone, it is important to understand that we must do our part and not just wait for others to do it all for us.

Sometimes people think they are living in time, when in actuality, they are killing time by wasting it away. Don't be one to wait and waste positivity. You should not waste another minute wishing and hoping you could do something. Be pro-active, and activate your doer gear into doing all that you can to achieve your goals. Don't merely leave things in other's hands, when you can do things yourself. God helps those who help themselves and others. Be a contributor to the cause and assist all those who are in need of your assistance. To give is to receive. When you give to others, you receive in the form of many blessings. To be a helper does not mean that you are inferior, but it does mean that you are at the top of your game. In being at the top of your game, allows you to understand and recognize that in helping others, you show more of a leader mentality that helps in achieving dreams and seeing them come into fruition.

A DAY IN THE LIFE OF POSITIVITY

As people, we have a responsibility to not sit back and wait on positivity to happen, but to maximize our effort by tapping into all that is positive in life. A whole lot of positivity is out there to embrace, that it is not necessary for anyone to focus on all that is negative. Negativity is restrictive on all levels, while positivity is nonrestrictive. In being positive, there are no restrictions. Being positive takes effort, but so does everything in life. We must do our part by thinking positive, and to reinforce our positive state of mind.

Each of us has a role to play in making life's daily journey a most positive experience for ourselves and others. A healthy and productive future is dependent on yours and others positive energy. We all share the responsibility to help each other. If you are reading this book, it shows that you are curious and have already made an effort to learn more about positive living. Realize that positivity is something that should not be waited on, but something that should be acted on. Once you understand this, take the initiative to pass the message along to all those souls who are willing to embrace your positive energy. Positive actions bring about positive results.

Hello Positivity

"To walk away does not always mean defeat; it sometimes means wisdom to know when it's time." We all have the gift of good-bye. When someone who is pulling you down chooses to leave, use your gift and say good-bye.

Is a blessing to, yet see another day, and it is a wonderful opportunity to get another chance to try to improve on all that was negative yesterday, and duplicate on all that is positive on this day. Life is a gift, so be thankful for the gift of life. Today signifies another opportunity to live and experience, so stop procrastinating on all that you want to do. There are many ways to put things off, but no one way to get time back. We are not living in eternity, as we know, life is not guaranteed. We only have this moment, so the

103

time is now to be proactive and begin doing what we want to do. Do not allow anyone to take away from this beautiful day. Each day brings an abundant of love. If anyone in your life attempts to prevent you from moving forward and seeing this love flourish, use your gift of being able to say good bye to that relationship. There are many different types of relationships, and they are not about hard ache, but about growth.

There are times in our lives, when we are forced to say good bye to love ones, (colleagues, family, friends, associates) but by no means should that stop you from moving forward. It is ok to walk away from toxic relationships. Anything or anyone who hampers your progression should not be allowed to have a voice in your positive movement. Feel free to say hello to positivity and know that in walking away does not mean defeat. Walking away sometimes means wisdom to know when it's time to move on. Do not wait until it is too late. Positivity is always willing to openly embrace all who wish to live in a day of the life of positivity. No one is perfect, and at times in life, we will fall along the way, but it is important to get back up and keep moving forward. One thing is to fall along the way on your own, and another is to allow others to pull you down. Again, do not give anyone that much power over you. You are in control of your path, so focus on the main objective of saying hello to positivity. Stay focus and keep that positive state of mind going.

Negative thoughts brings about low self-esteem and stress, so place a halt to anyone who attempts to bring negative thinking patterns that can have you in a low self-confidence funk. Remember, you have the power to use your gift of good bye to all that is toxic. Others can knowingly and at times, unknowingly attempt to bring negativity into your world, so it is essential that you learn to recognize negative thoughts and control them. You should also refuse them as you should not want others negative thoughts to occupy and clutter your mind. Your mind is not a garbage disposal, so don't allow others to dump their negativity onto you. Remember, you are in control of your thoughts, and not the thoughts of others. Use your wisdom of knowing that when someone refuses to go, you can take the initiative to walk away, and when someone who is pulling you down chooses to leave, use your gift and say good-bye. Either way, say good-bye, to all that is not positive.

Now is the time for Positivity

If not now, then when? There is no tomorrow unless you deal and address today. We always dream of tomorrow when living today. Though, you may expect to live a very long time, take advantage of your opportunities now. Don't put off family, friends, love, joy or even happiness for tomorrow. Inject Positivity into your life today and start living now.

If not now, then when? Stop finding excuses for not doing what you can and should be doing today. Excuses are what we say and use when we procrastinate for tomorrow on what we should be doing now. Instead of finding excuses, think of all the wonderful reasons why, you should say no to procrastination. Today should be your priority, as there is no better time to get started than now. Keep in mind that, unless you live out this day, tomorrow will not get here. This day is not promised to anyone, so it is essential to address and accomplish what we can today. Remember that tomorrow does not come, unless we experience and live today. We always dream of what we wish we could do tomorrow, when we should be focused on doing what we are able to do when living today. Dreams are wonderful, but they are more fulfilling when they are carried out to the fullest.

Even though, you may expect to live a very long time, take advantage of your opportunities today. Stop procrastinating and don't worry about making mistakes because that is part of life. We live to learn, and we learn when we live. We are humans and will make mistakes along the way. Just because, you have had set backs in life, it doesn't mean you stop living and let your dreams die. By taking action now, you can keep your dream alive. You should pursue what's in your heart. Know who you are and don't let anyone tell you different from what's in your heart. We are all Gems;

precious, different and rarest in form, but of great value, as we are worth all the wonders of life's many blessings.

It is a blessing to see this beautiful day. A new day brings us a new experience, and it is more gratifying when it is shared with others. Life's journey it's meant to be shared with others, so don't put off family, friends, love, joy, or even happiness for tomorrow when it can all be had today. Now is the time for positivity.

Many have the tendency to procrastinate and avoid doing what they should be doing in their lives. Procrastination can be caused by a variety of things, from fear, confusion, fatigued, depression, to lack of planning, but know that procrastination can be defeated if you put your mind to getting things done now. When we delay work, we delay achievement. Don't waste another moment procrastinating, and begin to use your time wisely by thinking of all the good things that can happen in your life if you stop impeding progression.   Inject positivity into your life today and start living now.

Positivity is the change to make

*Don't settle for tolerance and learn to change
what you don't like. Change your negative attitude
into a Positive attitude that helps you strive. Don't let,
good enough be good enough. Don't settle for
mediocrity. Positivity has no limit.*

Life is wonderful, and it is meant to be
maximize to the fullest. When it comes to anything in
life, that being love, relationships, friendship, career, or
opportunity, no one should settle. Settling means
routine, and we can enjoy life, when it is less routine.
Routine can be habitual and so mechanical, that it
dominates and consumes so much of our lives that most
of us are not enjoying life as much as we should be. At
times, it is important to get out of our mental assigned
box and explore as much as we can out of life.

Do not do things just because everyone else is doing it; do it, because that's what's in your heart. Do not let others use guilt, shame, denial, lies, or any other negative feeling to deter you from being the best you can be. If you adopt a loving attitude and accept self for who you are, there is nothing that you cannot accomplish. You must dedicate and put your mind into it. Transformation of self begins from within. Help others by contributing to their growth, and not use retribution against them for their lack of growth. Healing and love can be achieved when we are able to forgive others, and we can accept embracing ourselves.

Sometimes we struggle with what's ideal and what's real. We tend to create this ideal image of self and things around us. We think of how we want to be, and the way we wish things around us to be. For many, fantasy can become part of one's reality. Learn to accept but do not settle. Don't settle for tolerance and learn to change what you don't like. You are in control of self, so pave the path for a positive change.

A DAY IN THE LIFE OF POSITIVITY

A negative attitude will only take you so far, but a positive attitude will help you strive.   Always make the extra effort to achieve and reach a positive state that will leave you at ease and peace with self.

A lot of times, we find ourselves wanting to do right, but we fail to follow on our intentions.   Don't settle on only thinking on the positive things you could do, but act on your positive intentions by doing right. If we adopt a positive view, one of positive intentions, action and accomplishment, then we can positively move forward.   Physically, we live in the present. Unfortunately, many people live in the past mentally. Many simply do not know when to let go of the past, to appreciate the present, so it can lead to a gratifying future.   Learn to let go of negativity, and know, that positivity is the change to make.

By taking a stance, you say no to settling. Either turn around your negative situation or turn away from your negative situation.   Life is about options, approach and possibilities. Unless, you are willing to step up to the plate and take chances, don't expect change. Potential is great, but you need to put it into kinetic (action) to succeed. Don't let, good enough be good enough. Don't settle for mediocrity. Positivity has no limit.

Positivity brings optimism

No apology needed when one is true to self, but when wrong to others, own up to your mistake and share the lesson learned. No one is perfect, so always give yourself and others a chance at correction and redemption. Positivity brings about optimism. Keep it Positive and maximize your true calling.

Life's journey takes us into the unknown, but it all works out with optimism. In remaining optimistic about life, you will find your own way through life's struggles and lessons along the way. Life is about living and learning, so it is important not to be afraid to experience the manifestation of your potential.

As people, we should always strive to do right. Many times, we fail to carry out right, and instead, do wrong. Know that when doing wrong, it is not the end of the world. Though doing wrong is not right, you can always redeem yourselves with positive action. Reinforce positivity in all that you do. One way to do a positive act would genuinely be to apologize to others when wrong has been done. Keep in mind that if true to self, no apology is needed, but when wrong to others, own up to your mistake and don't forget to share the lesson learned. Don't allow pride to get in the way of doing right.

In life's journey, we should not miss an opportunity to do a good deed. We should all be firm believers in doing good deeds, as we are not in this life journey alone. We are all compassionate and naturally kind people, but we don't always allow that beauty within us to come out. Let all that beauty out, as positivity is contagious in the highest of way. If we all make out our mind to do good, we would see a chain reaction of doing one good, then two and so on. If we all practice this trend of doing good deeds, the vibes of this world would be kinder, gentler, and loving. Let's focus our energy more on all that's positive, as opposed to all that is negative. Let's be more of givers than that of takers. Focus on what you can do for others and do good deeds as often as time permits.

While enjoying life's journey, you should not get drawn into society's narcissistic way of believing that it's all about you. Listen to what those around you are saying. Pay attention to their needs. Sharing is caring. When opportunity arises, give heed by making a difference in someone else's life. No one is perfect, give yourself and others, a chance at correction and redemption.

After making lots of mistakes in life, we tend to love ourselves, but at times, refuse to forgive others for one mistake. Forgiveness is lighter on the soul than not forgiven could ever be. The feeling of holding on to grudge is too much of a burden for anyone to carry before it begins to jeopardize one's state of mind.

Learn to forgive and enjoy peace of mind.   Keep it positive to maximize, and live your true calling. Positivity brings optimism.

Positivity reigns supreme

Positivity and negativity are like two hungry lions. The one that gets fed the most, survives. If you want to live in harmony, you must feed your mind the Positive nourishment that it needs. Start by feeding it peace, humility, self-control, respect, patience, forgiveness, and love. Allow Positivity to reign supreme, within your savannah.

If you start the day speaking negative, keep thoughts of failure or believe that it's not going to be, then don't be surprised to see a beautiful day turn into a day of disarray. In other words, we are what we know, speak and reinforce. One should always feed their mind an enormous dosage of positive energy. Positivity and negativity are like two hungry lions, and the one that gets fed the most, survives. Believe that positivity will reign supreme, and it will. Cut the cord to that negative mental state and put out positive energy that would have you in a positive state of mind.

To live in a positive state is to live in harmony. If you want to live in harmony, you must feed your mind the positive nourishment that it needs. Starve your mind of negativity, while feeding it an abundance of positivity. Start by feeding it peace, humility, self-control, respect, patience, forgiveness, and love. When peace consumes you, it freely allows you to express your thoughts, and embrace your belief. A peaceful mind keeps you focus to remain optimistic and never lose hope. It teaches to live in the present moment, as tomorrow is not promised to anyone. Humility is when you are naturally modest and courteously respectful of others. Rather than allowing it to be about yourself, you allow it to be about others. In helping others, you help yourself. Like the world, our life goes around. What we do today seems to return to us in some fashion later on in the future.

A DAY IN THE LIFE OF POSITIVITY

Live for today, but keep in mind that today prepares us for what we may face tomorrow. Today's decisions affect how we live moving forward. In understanding this, one should always surround themselves with positive people that provide a loving vibe where you can grow in harmony. A sign of growth is when we recognize that we need help and lovingly embrace a positive outlook that have us living harmoniously.

Just like a Lion, you should reign supreme within your space. A good start would be to ensure that what you think, say, feel and do are aligned in a positive way. When there is harmony with our words, thoughts, feeling and actions, we experience an inner and outer sense of peace. In having inner peace, others can see it through our outer reflection. Allow others to see and feel that positive energy, just as you were able to see and learn it from others. We are not in this alone. Just like a Lion needs a prey to survive, we need knowledge and understanding to improve on all that allows us to live a healthy, fulfilling and positive life.   Allow the positive Lion within you to reign supreme, within your savannah.   You are the true king of your jungle.

Sharing is Positive

Everyone has something to offer that no one else can give, so take the time to make a difference. Give and make an impact. Don't just make your own life better, but think about how you can make someone else's life better as well. We are all in this together. In sharing, everyone gains.

Whether you are a doctor, lawyer, teacher, pilot, police, fireman, electrician, accountant, housekeeper, librarian, or unemployed, we all have something to offer the world that no one else can give. We are all unique in our own way, and that within itself is a blessing. We are all blessed to have options, so instead of nitpicking on the things that you currently may not have, take the time to make a difference in your life and that of those around you. In whatever you do, always give it a 100% effort. Anything short of giving it your best, it's unacceptable. Do not settle for average because no one is average. We were placed on this earth with a purpose. Whether you know it or not, we are all here for a reason, and we all have a purpose to serve in life. There are no coincidences in our being. Don't allow your special purpose to go to waste and maximize it by contributing to life's positive causes. There are many causes to contribute so pick one and have fun in adding to the positive movement. We can feed the hungry, help someone get a job, provide clothes to the bared, provide shelter to the homeless, teach the uneducated, or provide a map to those who may be lost. In anything that you choose, don't expect anything in return, and ensure to do everything with love in your heart. You will be repaid with the joy of watching those you have helped overcome obstacle. You will be able to see them with a sense of relief and gratitude in their eyes. We all fall short at times, but it is crucial to get back up and try again. Always strive to give it your best.

A DAY IN THE LIFE OF POSITIVITY

Give and make an impact by positively sharing.
Give of yourself and extend a hand to anyone who
needs it. Don't only focus on yourself, but think of
how you can make someone else's life better. In
extending and helping others, you make a positive
impact. Don't believe that you don't have anything to
share with anyone else. There are many non material
ways to help others. A perfect way is to share a smile.
Do not underestimate the power of a smile. You may
be surprised at the impact that a single smile can have
on someone else's life. Another way to help someone
else is by listening. Some people simply want an outlet
to vent. A soul who would listen without prejudice or
judgment can go a long way. The joy of life comes in
sharing positive light with those who want it.

In helping someone else, we also help ourselves.
Always remember, we are all in this together. No one
should ever have to be alone. Having success is great,
but success is nothing, when you don't have someone in
your life to share it with. Success by its lonesome is an

empty and lonely feeling.   If we develop the mindset to help another soul, we can progress as a whole.

Positivity should be shared, as sharing is positive.   We are all in this together; and remember, that in sharing, we all gain.